RSA:NC

RSA NEW CONTEMPORARIES
3-21 APRIL 2010

The Royal Scottish Academy has a proud tradition of promoting excellence in contemporary art in Scotland. Led by eminent artists and architects it supports the creation, understanding and enjoyment of the visual arts through exhibitions, artist opportunities and related educational talks and events. Re-establishing itself as a leading organisation for the visual arts in Scotland, it has successfully garnered a reputation for the strength of its engaging and diverse exhibitions and the fantastic opportunities it offers both established and emerging artists.

Published for the exhibition at
The Royal Scottish Academy of Art & Architecture
The Mound, Edinburgh, Scotland, EH2 2EL
www.royalscottishacademy.org

CONTE

INTRODUCTION

JOYCE W CAIRNS RSA

In Pat Barker's book 'Life Class' she describes a typical exchange between Henry Tonks and a student at the Slade in the spring of 1914, just before the outbreak of the First World War:
'For God's sake man, look at that arm. Its got no more bones in it than a sausage. Your pencil's blunt, your easel's wobbly, you're working in your own light and you seem to have no grasp of human anatomy at all – what is the point?'

Roll on the years to 1971 when the RSA Student Competition involved the selection of three painting students from each of the four Scottish art schools. We spent a week in Edinburgh College of Art producing a life painting and a composition. Brushes were synchronised at 9am and put down again on the stroke of 5.00. It seems extraordinary given the evolution of modernism through the preceding years, that a life painting was still the necessary indicator of quality in an emerging painter. There was only one prize awarded, The Carnegie Travelling Scholarship of £150, which in my case funded a whole summer in Italy.

Over the years the competition has had many changes and at one time also included third year students. All had to submit a framed drawing as well as a further work in their own discipline. For several years following this prizes were allocated from an open submission in which every work was guaranteed a place on the wall. The redesigned competition, now known as RSA New Contemporaries, was successfully inaugurated in 2009. In all new ventures there are always a few teething problems to overcome but then regular revision should prevent stagnation.

As Convener it was a fascinating, if not gruelling experience particularly given the short time between the various degree shows from which our artists were selected. It was however a privilege to be able to create an exhibition with such an open agenda. Of course I was not alone in this, and I am grateful for the invaluable contribution made by my fellow selectors from the Academy: Michael Agnew, Michael Docherty, Professor Ian Howard, Michael Visocchi and Arthur Watson, each of whom worked with two members of staff from each of Scotland's five fine art departments. The whole process was facilitated by Colin Greenslade and the Programme Team at the Royal Scottish Academy who liaised with the colleges and subsequently with the selected students. The Academicians on the selection also formed my hanging committee. In all, we looked at 343 fine art students - film makers, photographers and installation artists along with painters, sculptors and printmakers. Of these we selected 52, while the Architecture Convenor, Richard Murphy, worked closely with staff in the six schools of architecture on their selection. I would also like to thank staff from the colleges who, for the first time in our publication, have put the work of the graduates into context: Ray Mackenzie of Glasgow School of Art; Gina Wall of Moray School of Art; Jon Blackwood & Euan McArthur of Duncan of Jordanstone College of Art & Design; Gordon Brennan of Edinburgh College of Art; Alexandra M. Kokoli of Gray's School of Art and Richard Murphy RSA.

Given the ever-expanding range of influences and fields of activity that effect current practice in fine art and architecture, one hopes that an exhibition such as this will highlight the real qualities that are evident in the graduates of 2009. As always the range, imagination and fresh unselfconscious exuberance of much of this work leaves one feeling humble and sometimes rather pedestrian. Artistic maturity can of course bring its own restraints and predictable mannerisms, so it is like a breath of fresh air to be challenged by this new generation of artists.

Although we have asked some students for specific pieces to underpin the show, it is nonetheless a gamble, as the majority will have created something new with several works bearing little relation to those in their degree shows. Of course many of last year's graduates will already have had some exciting opportunities, but for others RSA New Contemporaries will have given them a focus for new work, and one which offers an invaluable and unique opportunity to exhibit in this magnificent professional venue, the chance for public engagement and the resultant publicity in both press and exhibition publication. For the public, the art world and aspiring Scottish art students this exhibition will provide an unrivalled opportunity to view some Scotland's most promising graduates.

Although the Academy itself has long ceased to be a teaching institution many of its members continue to teach in the schools of art and architecture and I continue to believe that one of the real strengths of the RSA is its engagement and support for emerging artists through this exhibition, the RSA John Kinross Scholarships to Italy, The Barns-Graham Travel Award, The Stevenston Award and many other prizes, awards and opportunities.

Joyce W Cairns RSA RSW
Exhibition Convener
RSA New Contemporaries 2010

EXHIBITO

SELECTED FROM THE 2009 DEGREE SHOWS

FINE ART DUNCAN OF JORDANSTONE COLLEGE OF ART & DESIGN
Omar Zingaro Bhatia
Jamie Fitzpatrick
Chloe Gough
Martin Hill
Astrid Leeson
Emma McIntyre
Georgia Murray
Jessica Ramm
Jonathan Richards
Carolyn Scott
Karen Skillen

FINE ART EDINBURGH COLLEGE OF ART
Alexander Allan
Magdalena Blasinska
Richard Bracken
Christopher Bryant
Kirstyn Cameron
Ernesto Canovas
Toby Cooke
Ben Fielding
Catriona Gilbert
Chris Mackie
Rachel Maclean
Tom Nolan
Catriona Reid
Peter Williams

FINE ART GLASGOW SCHOOL OF ART
Louis Guy
Sarah Hendry
David Jacobs
August Krogan-Roley
Michael Lacey
Harriet Lowther
Julia McKinlay
Yngvild Mehren
Laura Moss
Catriona Munro
Veronika Pausova
Eleanor Royle
Maximillian Slaven
Max Swinton
Fiona Weir
Rachel Wright

FINE ART GRAY'S SCHOOL OF ART
Andy Cumming
Jenny Hood
Gregor Morrison
Matthew Pang
Jacqueline Shortland
Scott Simpson
Alice Spicer
Richard Watson

FINE ART MORAY SCHOOL OF ART
Janet Gordon
Selena S. Kuzman

ARCHITECTURE
EDINBURGH COLLEGE OF ART
Klas Hyllen

MACKINTOSH SCHOOL OF ARCHITECTURE
Jonathan Middleton
Jon Morrison

SCOTT SUTHERLAND SCHOOL OF ARCHITECTURE & BUILT ENVIRONMENT
Greig Penny
Sara Russell

UNIVERSITY OF DUNDEE
Cameron McEwan

UNIVERSITY OF EDINBURGH
Piotr Lesniak

UNIVERSITY OF STRATHCLYDE
Andrew Campbell

DUNCAN OF JORDANSTONE COLLEGE OF ART & DESIGN

UNIVERSITY OF DUNDEE

FOREWORD BY JON BLACKWOOD & EUAN McARTHUR

ARTISTS

Omar Zingaro Bhatia

Jamie Fitzpatrick

Chloe Gough

Martin Hill

Astrid Leeson

Emma McIntyre

Georgia Murray

Jessica Ramm

Jonathan Richards

Carolyn Scott

Karen Skillen

DUNCAN OF JORDANSTONE COLLEGE OF ART & DESIGN

JON BLACKWOOD, LECTURER & HEAD OF HISTORY AND THEORY
EUAN MCARTHUR, SENIOR LECTURER IN HISTORY AND THEORY

The broad themes that characterise the work of any group of new artists will change according to the rapidly-shifting focus of a twenty-four hour news cycle-driven culture, and the subjects and objects it briefly spotlights before flitting, just as unexpectedly, elsewhere. The neuroses and obsessive preoccupations of such a society can often produce two consecutive graduate cohorts with seemingly radically different interests, and means of delivering those interests with a lasting impact to their audiences.

However this group of artists, who studied Fine Art at Dundee, concern themselves with themes that long predate our current age. They variously address the human portrait and its limitations, the process of making art as a subject in itself, and the systems of knowledge by which we interpret the world around us. In some there is a pronounced tendency towards fantasy and invented mythology, a turning inwards on the resources of the imagination, which also touches on allegory. An interest in materials, process and systems marks the work of another grouping, taking a broadly formal turn though not to narrowly formalist ends.

We all have our internal narratives of self, but Carolyn Scott's photography takes off from the insight that people's life-stories may seem unremarkable to them though not to others. Equally, our tendency to amass memorabilia is, she fears, threatened by dissolution into the temporality of digital media, the sheer fecundity of which deprives them of the value of the unique, treasureable images of the traditional family album. So, proposing that to value the present we have to value the past, her current project involves the creation of "personal archives" that combine photography, text and sound recordings, as un-staged and 'natural' as possible to catch the particular reality of the individual. The particular is also central to Chloe Gough's paintings. How we reveal ourselves to others though body, posture and dress, and how we scan them in others for signs of character and personality, has led her to an indirect, allusive approach to the painted portrait in which the element we most expect, the face and its returned or averted gaze, is denied. Instead we are given almost abstract, low-key, visual cues. Identity emerges despite its seeming denial. Omar Bhatia's installation, laden with imagery and curiosities, plays with the stereotypical perceptions of the Victorian dilettante and the cyberspace flaneur. His work treads a high wire between fact and fiction, and a refusal to be confined by his "cultural" identity, instead holding it up to gentle self-mocking humour, ironzing the notion of identity as destiny whether self-given or ascribed by others.

'Identity' is connected to notions of boundedness, to transgress which is to enter the mythic space of the hybrid and the monster. So, in a literary way, one might argue, but transgenics would see it otherwise. Far from being against nature, combining genes from different species is an application of nature to ends that, while raising moral issues, nature doesn't preclude. Jamie Fitzpatrick locates his 'Unnatural History Museum' at this juncture of science, art and myth, and of an imagined past and future. Combining taxidermy and different materials (such as bronze, plaster and fibreglass) with technical facility (and an astute understanding of anatomy and the classification of species) his beasts engage the fascination for the fantastic and terrible. They propose the emergence of a new transgenic natural history of the future, in which creatures (recallling H.G. Wells' forebodings in The Island of Dr. Moreau) have acquired a tragic quasi-human pathos. One animal beyond all others in which myth and reality are hard to separate (at least in art) is the bull. It is the heroic absent presence of Emma McIntyre installation, alluded to by lance-like chrome poles which spring from floor and walls. They define an open arena of aggressive, disrupted space, enacting what she calls a "tactile violence" on the encircled viewer's emotions. Her identification with the bull expresses her own struggle to create in a world which increasingly regards creativity for its own sake (as opposed to some utilitarian end) with scepticism, if not outright contempt.

Personal identification with mythic subject matter is part too of Martin Hill's tactile paintings in which an interest in German expressionism and classical and renaissance myth is synthesised. Their origin is partly autobiographical but they find their form through essentially allegorical subjects from literature. This might invite the suspicion of bombast, but any such risk is disarmed by their acute pictorial and painterly good sense and dead-pan wit. Allegory (often entwined with myth) is far from being an outmoded trope in contemporary art. Jessica Ramm makes metaphysical machines that allegorize the human condition as founded on cycles of desire, hope and frustration. They suggest an unlikely synthesis of the work of Calder, Arp and Fischli & Weiss, but an allusion to Duchamp too is unmistakeable. Clearly, she delights in the dance of absurdity and futility and in something else. To merely make their point there would be no need of antique cogs, heavy levers and sturdy frames to support wildly delicate glass jars, wire pulleys and flickering electrical filaments (plus the minuscule tapping of a dozen metal beaks). Redundancy and excess are surely intended to satirize and celebrate pointless labour, for celebratory pointless labour is, after all, a decent definition of art.

Mechanical and organic systems have often provided metaphors that mythologize the state, but real bureaucratic, political and physical systems pervade urban space. Yet out of reach of authority, social space is pervaded by what Michel de Certeau described as "the ruses and combinations of powers that have no readable identity". The psychic currents that course through the spaces of the city are the source of Astrid Leeson's work. In a sense, they are her medium because her structures register her subjective responses to place, expressed through compounds of found objects, casts (the echoes of objects), printing and drawing. Their heterogeneity and simultaneity offer a richly allusive visual language that evokes both the hard (material) and soft (immaterial) city of everyday life.

Jonathan Richards' painting, which appears at first glance to be an intervention in the territory of minimalism, conceals subtlety and ambiguity beneath its pristine surfaces. Process is key to his practice - the continual sense of soft layering and addition, scrambling the viewer's initial sense of finality. Rather, Richards' work, which may appear impenetrable, is an invitation to imagine the process by which these objects were made, and to evaluate the experience we have of them in their particular setting. Fascinated by the effects that light and shadow have on his finished works, he takes great care in siting them within each different gallery space. This, then, is no exercise in self-referential aesthetics, but each new exhibition of these works forms part of a visual and experiential journey. Parallel to this, Georgia Murray's paintings explore the relationship between colour, emotion and time. Her paintings consist of different narrative fragments within an overall brightly coloured image, as she explores the evocative qualities of colour in terms of memory and personal history. Murray's exploration of colour in the medium of paint, its effects in a confined pictorial space, and the response of the viewer, are analysed with an intensity similar to that in Richards' work. A uniquely personal response to the natural world is also unfolded in Karen Skillen's exquisite silverpoint and gesso works. Her approach is not to copy processes and systems she observes in nature; rather, she develops the dynamic, permutating series of visual structures that articulate her surfaces as a means of responding to natural processes and rhythms of growth, change and decay. Subtleties of light and the serendipity found in nature underpin these complex and multi-layered pictorial analogues.

OMAR ZINGARO BHATIA

GRADUATED: DUNCAN OF JORDANSTONE COLLEGE OF ART & DESIGN

www.zingaromar.blogspot.com

Omar's Spuriosity Shop [2009] Image courtsey of Ross Fraser Mclean

JAMIE FITZPATRICK

GRADUATED: DUNCAN OF JORDANSTONE COLLEGE OF ART & DESIGN

Unnatural_history_museum@hotmail.com

Images from left: **Tell me, what do you see?** [2010] Life size taxidermy
Oudry's Game [2010] Life size taxidermy, bronze & string. Photography by Ross Fraser McLean

CHLOE GOUGH

GRADUATED: DUNCAN OF JORDANSTONE COLLEGE OF ART & DESIGN
www.chloegough.net

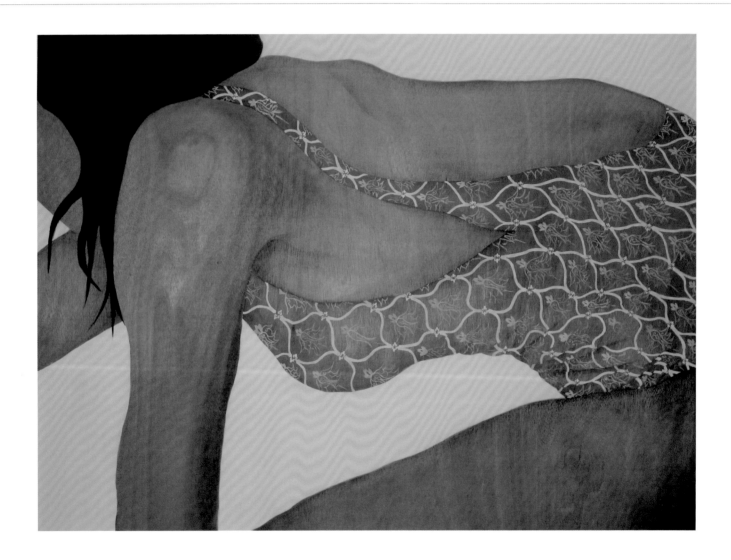

Reach [2009] Water based wood stain, ink, acrylic and pencil, 72 x 101cm

MARTIN HILL

GRADUATED: DUNCAN OF JORDANSTONE COLLEGE OF ART & DESIGN

martin_hill@live.com

Goat I [2009] Oil on board, 28 x 35.2cm

ASTRID LEESON

GRADUATED: DUNCAN OF JORDANSTONE COLLEGE OF ART & DESIGN
samandasti@aol.com

Installation [2009] Plaster, steel, concrete, approximate floor space 3 x 5 x 5m

EMMA McINTYRE

GRADUATED: DUNCAN OF JORDANSTONE COLLEGE OF ART & DESIGN

www.emmamcintyre.blogspot.com

Above All, Thanks to the Bulls [2009] Photographer Wes Kingston

GEORGIA MURRAY

GRADUATED: DUNCAN OF JORDANSTONE COLLEGE OF ART & DESIGN

theabyssofpaint@live.co.uk

Wings are for birds [2009] Acrylic, oil, gloss, fluorescent pigment, marker pen, 180 X 183cm

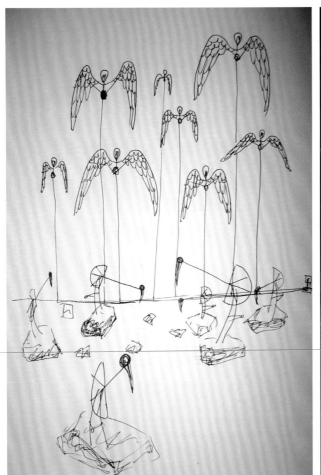 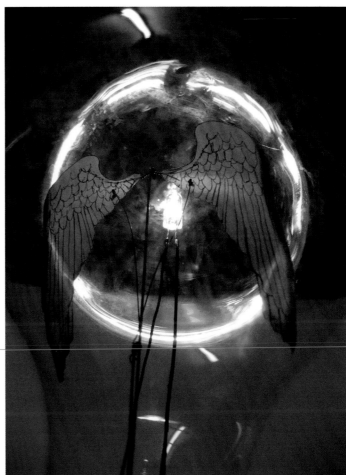

Images from left: **Project overview sketch** [2010]. Pen and ink
Ikaros Bulb [2010] Glass, tin, electrical components, 40 x 20cm

JONATHAN RICHARDS

GRADUATED: DUNCAN OF JORDANSTONE COLLEGE OF ART & DESIGN
www.jpfrichards.com

Images from left: **Duncan** [2009]; **Edward** [2009]
Paint skin stretched onto linen and board, circa 150 x 200 cm

CAROLYN SCOTT

GRADUATED: DUNCAN OF JORDANSTONE COLLEGE OF ART & DESIGN

casfife@lycos.com

Albs. Material Light Series [2007] Giclee printed photographs mounted on aluminium, 42 x 55.5cm

KAREN SKILLEN

GRADUATED: DUNCAN OF JORDANSTONE COLLEGE OF ART & DESIGN
karen_skillen@live.co.uk

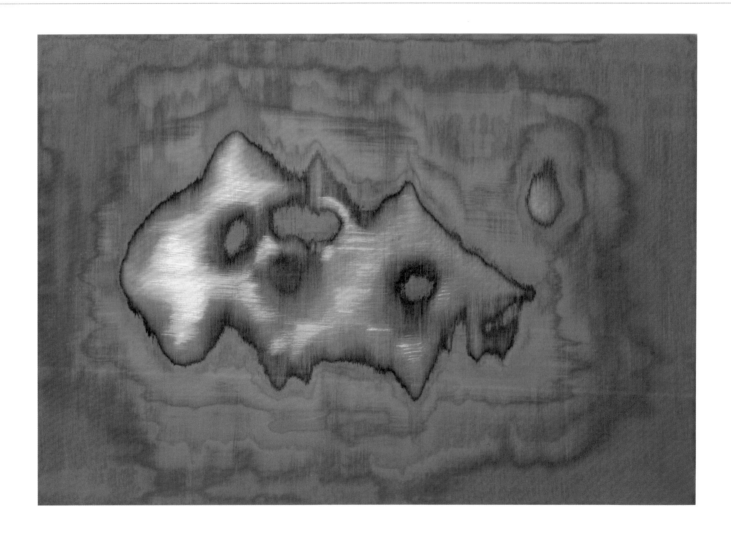

#5 [2009] Gesso & sheet-metal drawings on board, 31 x 45cm

EDINBURGH COLLEGE OF ART

FOREWORD BY GORDON BRENNAN

ARTISTS

Alexander Allan
Magdalena Blasinska
Richard Bracken
Christopher Bryant
Kirstyn Cameron
Ernesto Canovas
Toby Cooke
Ben Fielding
Catriona Gilbert
Chris Mackie
Rachel Maclean
Tom Nolan
Catriona Reid
Peter Williams

EDINBURGH COLLEGE OF ART

GORDON BRENNAN, ASSOCIATE HEAD, SCHOOL OF ART

The nature of an exhibition such as this brings in to question just how such a group of artists come together. The obvious point of departure here is that these artists were peers at Edinburgh College of Art. They were, like all students thrown together through chance, through their choice of specialisms, through their surname, through their shared studio space(s), through shared interests, common language, a sense of curiosity and more recently being selected for the RSA New Contemporaries.

All these things were never considered as some manipulative experiment in social engineering, but by the nature of an art college education, the proximity and intimacy of the studio practice generates a unique learning community. Relationships are founded on shared interests, the questioning of values and above all a generosity of spirit and mutual respect. The nature of the individual's identity is partially formed by the investment and involvement in shared experience, where peer support makes a significant difference to expectations and production.

The study and pursuit of artistic knowledge can be a solitary experience, there is never the applause when it comes right, for every solution generates a new doubt or a question. The study and the making of art share these problems but unlike other areas of study the studio model engenders a democratization and socialisation of knowledge and experience.

Art education, is a unique form of learning, it is structured but part of that structure is about having a space, the studio is a physical space but more importantly there is a mental space that permits opportunities, a place to "work out what to do when you don't know what to do" and a place "to see what happens if.... ?

Through this, students are empowered to take charge of their study, to in a way, shape a curriculum that is built on existing individual interests and attributes, on a partnership between themselves, their peers and staff.

The artist or art student can create work autonomously but the reality is there is always a high degree of collaboration, either in the day-to-day production or in the fact that the work will, upon completion, more often than not operate alongside that of other artists. The work changes, new relationships and dialogues are formed. The deep specialist knowledge gained within the creation of the individual work is tested against the broader context. The artists views the work whilst it is being made in a very particular way and also when it is complete the artist becomes a viewer with a different perception than that of the gallery audience.

The acts of negotiation that are embedded in making art form some of the sophisticated mechanisms that define art practice. From the individuals questioning of concept, constant analysis and reflection, the challenging of perceived knowledge through to the more collaborative, networking and communication strategies employed, all provide the student (and the artist) with a unique skill set that becomes second nature and, unfortunately, occasionally taken for granted.

By shaping their own work they become involved in an intense awareness of self and a high level of agency; by engaging in this activity, they are in fact participating in the shaping and, or altering the world. This heightened self-awareness involved in individual practice provides access to the understanding of the complexities of the collective experience and to the sensibilities and concerns of others.

The student, artist is constantly moving from self-reflective isolation to being fully engaged in, and conscious of, the subtleties of other creative responses from their peers. As in the idea of the interdisciplinary student / artist first gaining the deep knowledge of their own specialism before being able to explore the boundaries and the surrounding territories, similarly the knowing of ones self allows a greater empathy with and the ability to contribute to the concerns of others.

The student artist, questions, explores, organises, recognizes phenomena pertinent to themselves but through an openness, a curiosity and a finely tuned level of receptiveness they are able to share and celebrate the uniqueness of experience and thus reshape collective knowledge.

The students who have installed work for this exhibition exemplified many of the above characteristics, all of them clearly grounded in their own practice with a deep knowledge of their own core values. As a year group they encompassed a great diversity of approaches and strategies. They were a group that also had a great sense of collective responsibility, very supportive and respectful but were also able to be critical of each other's practice.

It is possible to assume that these attributes are universal in higher education; we sometimes fail to recognize the uniqueness of an art college education. The studio discipline provides a laboratory that permits a very democratic community where subtle nuances of meaning, levels of complexity and doubt become a creative discourse.

The making of good art, particularly the work we experience in this exhibition becomes an invitation to not only perceive the individuals perspective but to celebrate the differences that enrich our own perception of the world.

The work is complete when it reveals and illuminates the place where it comes from; in this case, from a group of dynamic, mischievous, poetic and intelligent ambassadors for Edinburgh College of Art.

ALEXANDER ALLAN

GRADUATED: EDINBURGH COLLEGE OF ART
www.alexallan.co.uk

Kiln 2 (Power Station - Ash Lagoons) East Lothian [2009] Abandoned bricks, dimensions variable

MAGDALENA BLASINSKA

GRADUATED: EDINBURGH COLLEGE OF ART

www.magdablasinska.com

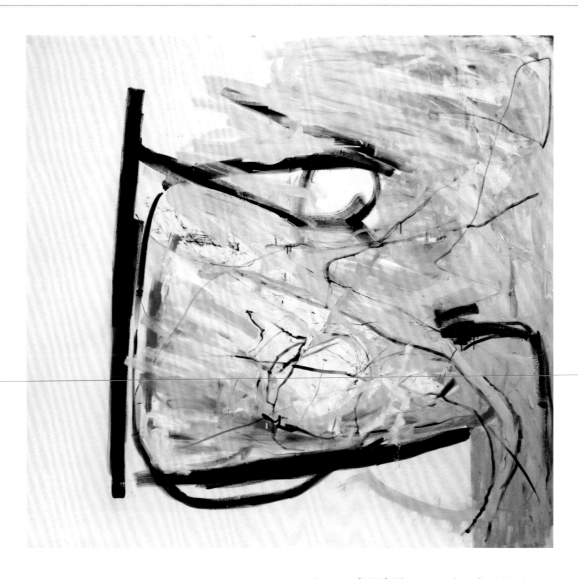

Operetta [2009] Oil, gesso and acrylic, 240 x 240cm

RICHARD BRACKEN

GRADUATED: EDINBURGH COLLEGE OF ART

rsbracken@hotmail.com

Images from left: **Ruin 1** [2009]; **Glen Dubh Lighe** [2008]

28

CHRISTOPHER BRYANT

GRADUATED: EDINBURGH COLLEGE OF ART

www.christopherbryant.co.uk

Blok M [2009] Installation, board, resin, acrylic. Photography by John McGregor

KIRSTYN CAMERON

GRADUATED: EDINBURGH COLLEGE OF ART
www.kirstyncameron.com

Untitled [2009] Resin, each approximately 10 x 10cm

ERNESTO CANOVAS

GRADUATED: EDINBURGH COLLEGE OF ART

www.ernestocanovas.com

Psycho Buildings [2009] Mixed media on board, 55 x 40cm

TOBY COOKE

GRADUATED: EDINBURGH COLLEGE OF ART

www.tobycooke.com

Images from left: **Monolith IX** [2009] Photograph, 40 x26cm; **Horizon XV** [2009] Mixed media on panel, 112 x 80cm

Tappy Tappy [2009] Piano hammers, pear wood.

CATRIONA GILBERT

GRADUATED: EDINBURGH COLLEGE OF ART
www.catrionagilbert.com

After Freya & Daedalus [2009] Feather Cloak. Photography James Haddrill

Running Through A Forest Wearing A Blindfold [2009] Digital film still

RACHEL MACLEAN

GRADUATED: EDINBURGH COLLEGE OF ART

www.rachelmaclean.com

Mother and Child [2009] Digital painting

Images from left: **Cacti Paradisum** [2009] Collage photocopies, 42 x 29.7cm; **Untitled** [2009] Found photograph

CATRIONA REID

GRADUATED: EDINBURGH COLLEGE OF ART
www.catrionareid.co.uk

Maquettes for RSA New Contemporaries project [2010] Paper models, mirrors, video & sound work, approximately 3 x 4m²

PETER WILLIAMS
GRADUATED: EDINBURGH COLLEGE OF ART
petercynanwilliams.blogspot.com

Bridge of uncertainties, North Wales [2009] Photograph, 15 x 10cm

GLASGOW SCHOOL OF ART

FOREWORD BY RAY McKENZIE

ARTISTS

Louis Guy

Sarah Hendry

David Jacobs

August Krogan-Roley

Michael Lacey

Harriet Lowther

Julia McKinlay

Yngvild Mehren

Laura Moss

Catriona Munro

Veronika Pausova

Eleanor Royle

Maximillian Slaven

Max Swinton

Fiona Weir

Rachel Wright

GLASGOW SCHOOL OF ART

RAY MCKENZIE, SENIOR LECTURER IN HISTORICAL AND CRITICAL STUDIES

In the predictably chaotic flurry of activity that accompanied the preparations for the GSA Degree Show in the summer of 2009, I doubt if the graduating students gave much thought to the significance of the year in which the event took place. And yet 2009 was a major milestone in the history of the School. By December of that year, the celebrated Mackintosh Building, the building in which their work was displayed and which is revered throughout the world as Charles Rennie Mackintosh's architectural 'masterwork', would be exactly 100 years old.

Equally predictable was the fact that this was something the School itself took very seriously, and no sooner had the by now former students vacated the premises than preparations were under way for an exhibition featuring, among other things, the work of some of their predecessors who had studied at the School during the period when the building was first occupied – a retrospective Degree Show, you might say, for 1909. Entitled The Flower and the Green Leaf, the show took its cue from Mackintosh's much-quoted assertion that 'art is the flower, life is the green leaf', and the intention was to go beyond merely displaying the sort of work that students were doing at that time, and to evoke the kind of lived experience they had as emergent artists studying in Glasgow at the dawn of a new century. It also provided an opportunity to understand better the values and aspirations that drove art education at that time, and to assess the distance we have come in both the practice of art and how it is taught. This was a time when, to put it crudely, painters produced paintings, sculptors made statues, printmakers stuck to their woodblocks and everyone strove to 'draw like an angel'. One corner of the show was especially revealing. Here we could see the School's plaster facsimile of the classical Greek statue of Apollo Sauroctonus juxtaposed with an exquisitely finished drawing of it in red chalk by a student named William Gray. It was difficult not to form the impression that life for art students in 1909 was,

though certainly no easier than it is for their counterparts today, a great deal more straight forward. Not only was the making of work carried out in the comfort zone of a strictly medium-specific practice, but the relevant technical skills were acquired in the equally clearly defined space bounded by the antique room on one side and the life class on the other. Whatever other difficulties the process of learning might have presented to the students of 1909, at least they knew where they were and precisely what was expected of them.

A quick mental flip between this and the work shown in the summer of 2009 reveals a massive process of change that has brought with it the dissolution of every kind of formal, technical and conceptual boundary, an attitude towards subject matter that declares open season on the world and all its works, the replacement of the 'life class' by life itself. In a word, freedom. And yet freedom brings its own constraints and its own hazards. Where the injunction used to be 'draw this, and do it like this', what we now say to our students is more like: 'OK, let's see you do something interesting'. It sounds easy, but in practice it is a very stiff challenge indeed.

So how did the class of 2009 respond to this challenge? Before I can answer this I must explain the difficulties the question involves. It is now February 2010, so that the text I am producing is suspended in a limbo-like space between two fixed points: the Degree Show itself, which took place seven months ago and is accessible to me now through little more than the faulty medium of memory; and the New Contemporaries show, which has still to be curated and which therefore nobody has yet seen. How does one negotiate such a space? Under the circumstances, the most reliable guide I have is the collection of short statements that each of the sixteen selected graduates has provided, outlining their concerns as artists and their intentions for the new show. As a modest thought experiment it occurred to me that it might be useful to undertake what sociologists call a 'content analysis' of what they had to say, plotting the ideas and concerns that appeared most frequently among their statements as one set of coordinates on a graph against a vertical checklist of their names. The result was, I freely admit, a statistically useless document, but an interesting one all the same. Here is a summary of my findings.

A recurring preoccupation was with lovingly re-presenting traces left behind by the lives of others (Laura Moss, Catriona Munro, August Krogan-Roley, Michael Lacey, Eleanor Royle), or the poetics of the everyday (Harriet Lowther, Veronika Pausova, David Jacobs). A variation of this was an obsession with the aesthetics of decay sought out in different forms of debris and detritus (Moss, Lacey, Royle), but which could equally well manifest itself in the exploration of various types of interior space, such as the domestic (Krogan-Roley) and the institutional (Max Slaven, Rachel Wright, Lowther, Royle,). For some there was a special sort of emotional resonance to be found in a building that has been abandoned for all human purposes (Moss, Krogan-Roley, Royle), while others sought a similar melancholy in the graveyard (Munro, Wright). In several cases the concern for the everyday gravitated naturally towards an interest in popular culture (Max Swinton, Sarah Hendry, Munro, Lowther, Lacey, Jacobs), sometimes with an emphasis on sexual politics (Hendry), sometimes through a confrontation with the unrelenting grittiness of urban experience (Munro).

On the matter of how these students positioned themselves within a broader historical and cultural context, the guiding references varied from the history or art itself (Lacey, Guy), sometimes combined with ancient mythology (Wright), to visions of a post-apocalyptic dystopian future (Moss, Munro). Cutting across this was a recurring engagement with various more abstract concerns, such as the binary opposition between culture and nature (Fiona Weir, Julia McKinlay, Yngvild Mehren), the essentially tragic aspect of human mortality (Moss, Lacey, Mehren), the realm of dreams and the numinous (Pausova, Krogan-Roley, Royle,Wright, Mehren) or a more general desire to penetrate beyond the contingent to what might be described as 'universal' values (Swinton, Krogan-Roley, Lowther).

More than half the statements had something to say about the writers' working method and their attitude towards the materials they deployed. The combined interest in popular culture and the traces of other people's lives led many to embrace the use of found objects and materials normally discarded as trash (Moss, Weir, Hendry, Royle, Mehren and possibly Munro), with only a very small number expressing an explicit interest in demonstrating anything that might resemble a traditional craft skill (Weir, McKinlay, Royle). As has been the case with GSA graduates for a number of years now, an interest in good old-fashioned narrative made a healthy showing (Moss, Krogan-Roley, Lacey, Wright, Guy, Swinton), while the commitment of several writers to the use of rigorous repetition as an organising principle suggests that the legacy of 1970s Conceptual Art retains its relevance today (Lowther, Slaven, Royle). But for me the biggest surprise – though here I am drawing more on my recollection of the show itself than the statements – was the amount of work that eschewed the current mixed-media orthodoxy to produce works that could be identified unambiguously as paintings or sculptures or photographs (McKinlay, Krogan-Roley, Lacey, Moss, Wright, Pausova, Guy, Mehern). In this respect at least, there was some continuity with what their forebears were doing in 1909.

I must ask you to make whatever you can of this crude attempt to interpret what is after all nothing more than a sheet of paper with a lot of crosses on it. The analysis is not of the work the students made but of what they had to say about it, which is a very different matter, and for those who did not see the GSA Degree Show itself this is unlikely to mean very much. By the time this text appears, however, the New Contemporaries show will have been curated, installed and opened to the public, and it will be interesting to see how much of this makes sense in the light of what these sixteen emergent artists, all of whom I last encountered as undergraduates, have done since departing from GSA.

It is always invidious when writing about student work to single out particular pieces for special mention, and indeed one of the reasons I have adopted a statistical approach here is to ensure that every one of the thirteen participants is properly name-checked. But at this remove from the event, the subjective workings of memory will inevitably have their way, and I would like to conclude by noting one or two of the works that made the most lasting impression on me. Among them are Julia McKinlay's sculptures, which were memorable for their straight-forwardly formal beauty, unimpeded by any theoretical concerns more abstruse than a desire to bring natural and artificial forms together and see how well they got on with each other. The results were exquisite. For their density of content, and the remarkable synchronisation of conceptual and technical concerns, the etchings of Ellie Royle – made on galvanised steel plates that had been removed from the windows of derelict buildings – had no equal in the entire show, while the brilliantly coloured but genuinely disturbing paintings of dystopian interiors by August Krogan-Roley clearly penetrated deeply enough into my psyche to remain there haunting me to this day.

For once, though, I find myself in agreement with verdict of the press. The great favourite of the journos last year, and the work that drew the most extensive coverage, was a piece called

The Big Thank You, by Hariet Lowther (cited above under the poetics of the everyday, institutional spaces, popular culture and Conceptual Art). This consisted of a wall-sized assembly of identically framed letters that the artist had sent over a period of time to people belonging to organisations that had either manufactured a product or provided a service from which she felt she had benefited. The range was huge and bizarre, extending from Maped paper clips to the Royal Bank of Scotland. Like much serial work that exploits difference in repetition, The Big Thank You grew in intellectual complexity the more strictly its single central idea was enforced, and the result was a witty and touching insight into the workings of consumerism. Lowther describes this 'perpetual project' as existing on the borderline between sincerity and sarcasm so it is difficult to be sure if the enterprise is anything other than a monumental bluff. But then its strength lies precisely in its ambivalence.

At the same time, the point about ambivalent meanings is that they mutate as circumstances change. In the seven months since we applauded Lowther's wit and the apparent candour with which she disclosed her habits as a consumer we have seen the credit crunch, the bank bailout and a re-configuring of our financial system in what can best be described as The Big Up Yours. A few weeks ago it was reported in The Times that some bright spark had written to the disgraced former boss of the RBS, Fred 'the Shred' Goodwin, to say how much he deplored the unfair criticism he and his banking colleagues had been made to suffer for their harmless little 'bonuses'. Goodwin, arrogant clod that he is, actually believed him, and replied to say how grateful he was that somebody appreciated the true value of his contribution to society. I wonder if Lowther will bring her 'perpetual project' up to date in the light of all this. A letter perhaps to the Student Loan Company? I look forward to finding out.

LOUIS GUY

GRADUATED: GLASGOW SCHOOL OF ART

Kinglouisprivatestudy.blogspot.com

The destruction of Cesena [2009] Oil on board, 200cm x 150cm

SARAH HENDRY

GRADUATED: GLASGOW SCHOOL OF ART
www.myspace.com/mitsymoonbeam

Lilies [2009] Colour digital print, 114x 84cm

DAVID JACOBS

GRADUATED: GLASGOW SCHOOL OF ART

davidsstuffandbits.blogspot.com

Giant Pinata Robot [2010] Animation still

AUGUST KROGAN-ROLEY

GRADUATED: GLASGOW SCHOOL OF ART
www.augustkroganroley.com

Ileum hearth [2009] Oil on canvas (diptych), 130 x 60cm

Dying Ghost [2010] Digital photograph

HARRIET LOWTHER

GRADUATED: GLASGOW SCHOOL OF ART
www.harrietlowther.com

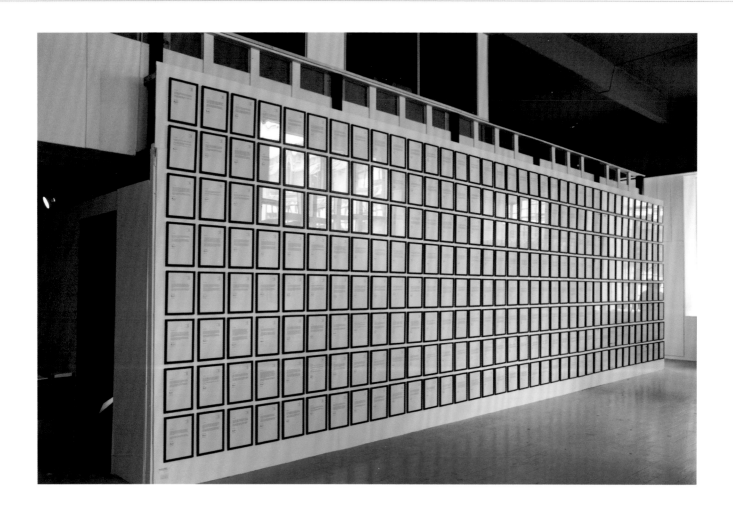

The Big Thank You Project [2009] Installation view, digital inkjet prints

Flamingo Landscape Mineral [2009] Mixed media, approx 5 x 4 x 4m

YNGVILD MEHREN

GRADUATED: GLASGOW SCHOOL OF ART

www.yngvildmn.foto.no

Garsjø - The Snow Land, Norway [2009] Photograph

LAURA MOSS

GRADUATED: GLASGOW SCHOOL OF ART

laura.moss@yahoo.co.uk

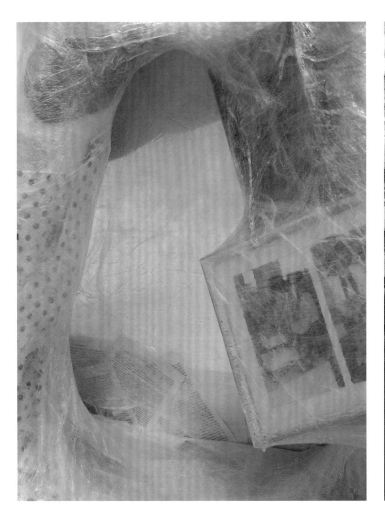 

Images from left:
Dropped in Flight III [2009] Mixed Media (found objects, cling film and resin), Dimensions variable approx. 145 x 45 x23cm
Then They Changed Their Minds and Let Go [2009] Digital Print , 170 x 80cm

CATRIONA MUNRO

GRADUATED: GLASGOW SCHOOL OF ART
www.catrionamunro.blogspot.com

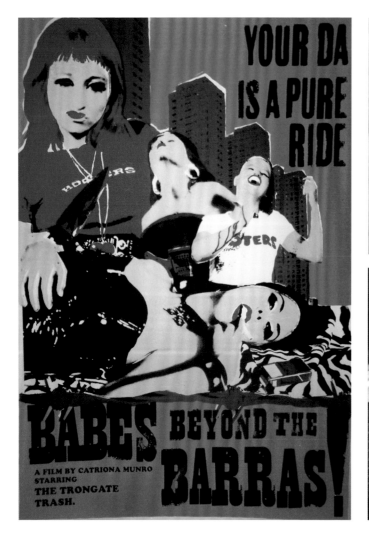

Images clockwise from left: **Babes beyond the Barras** [2009] Poster; **Babes beyond the Barras** [2009] Video Stills I & II

VERONIKA PAUSOVA
GRADUATED: GLASGOW SCHOOL OF ART
veronika_pausova@hotmail.com

Motel Room [2009] Oil on board

ELEANOR ROYLE

GRADUATED: GLASGOW SCHOOL OF ART
www.ellieroyle.com

The Impossible View No.3, 'Staff Quarters' [2009] Duo-tone photo etching, 108 x 104.5cm

Piece by Piece - Hayward Gallery, London [2009] C - Print, 50 x 60cm

MAX SWINTON

GRADUATED: GLASGOW SCHOOL OF ART
www.maximilianswinton.squarespace.com

Mr Fox [2009] Film still

FIONA WEIR

GRADUATED: GLASGOW SCHOOL OF ART

horsesandmonkeys@hotmail.com

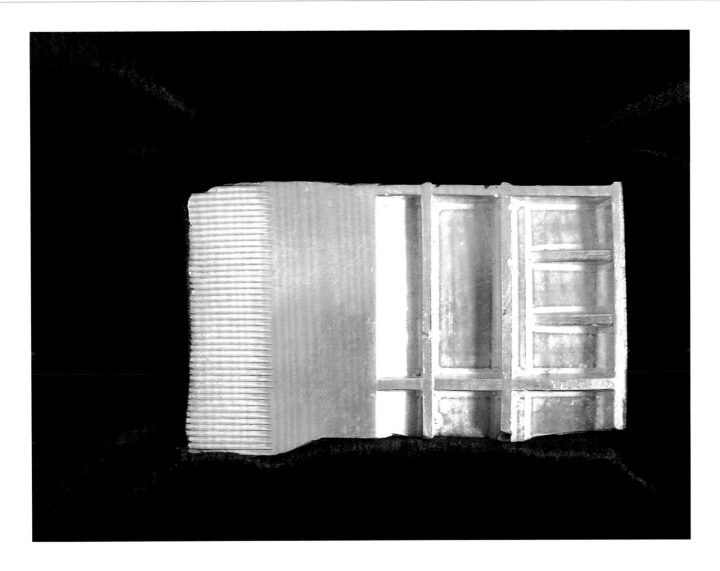

News from Nowhere [2009] Silver 5 x 1 x 9cm, oasis block, velvet

RACHEL WRIGHT

GRADUATED: GLASGOW SCHOOL OF ART

www.rachel-wright.com

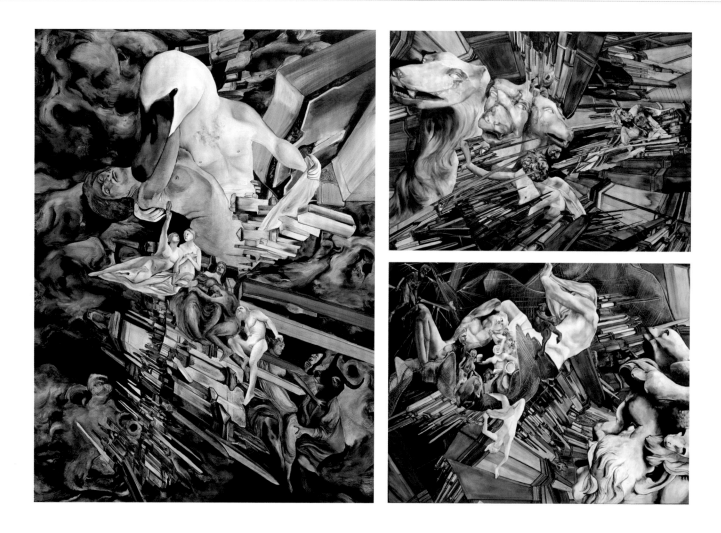

Image clockwise from left: **Swan Transformation** [2009] Oil on board, 100 x 75cm
Cerberus [2009] Oil on board, 80cm x 110; **Bacchus To The Future** [2009] Oil on board, 80cm x 110

GRAY'S SCHOOL OF ART
ROBERT GORDON UNIVERSITY, ABERDEEN
FOREWORD BY ALEXANDRA M KOKOLI

ARTISTS

Andy Cumming

Jenny Hood

Gregor Morrison

Matthew Pang

Jacqueline Shortland

Scott Simpson

Alice Spicer

Richard Watson

GRAY'S SCHOOL OF ART

ALEXANDRA M KOKOLI, LECTURER IN CRITICAL AND CONTEXTUAL STUDIES

Self-described as 'the UK's most northerly art school',1 Gray's School of Art has a particular reputation to live up to – or challenge. Its location is often highlighted because it is about much more than geography: it suggests ruggedness, isolation but also a certain pride in holding the fort for art and culture in an otherwise not altogether conducive environment. Aberdeen, an international city that hides it well, is regularly compared to (and contrasted with) the so-called central belt of Scotland, which affirms its marginal location and implied marginalisation. It is a matter of public knowledge and consternation among those involved in the arts that Aberdeen has not experienced the cultural regeneration that many British post-industrial urban centres have, since it is still industrial and widely reliant on the oil reserves of the North Sea. Nevertheless, the veracity of the connotations of 'the North' matters less than their considerable sway over the public imagination. This virtual positioning of the city and its art school 'on the edge' inspires a range of self-representations, attitudes and ways of being that range from the wilfully insular to the enabling. After all, 'on the edge' can also refer to a model for interdisciplinarity and, more importantly, a meaningful engagement between higher education, the visual arts and the public sphere: 'a space of constant change, a threshold of new experience, with the potential for creative transformation'.2 It is primarily the advantages of this positioning that are in evidence in the work of the RSA's selection from Gray's. Relatively sheltered from passing trends and freer from the pressures of the art market, it is no accident that these graduates share a strong interest in the interface between nature and culture, talent and training,

ingenuousness and institutionalisation, with some of the work developing in a distinctly neo-primitivist/ post-naïve strands.

The joyful and vaguely menacing monochrome woodcuts of Andy Cumming are the clearest example of this neo-primitivist vein. Neither fully figurative nor abstract but both, Cumming's looping lines and stout yet fragile forms call to mind real and imaginary animals, stuffed toys and machinery, in equal measure. As in the work of Klee and Dubuffet, the evocation of children's creativity is here an argument for a calculated retreat from the binds of aesthetic and conceptual conventions, its simplicity only a sheen beneath which unfolds a knowing and fruitful experimentation. In some prints, black and white, positive and negative space are reversed, challenging the fundamental division between figure and background. Jenny Hood's multimedia practice invokes the boundaries between nature and culture through taxidermy. Her interest in this technique is not merely academic, although the history of taxidermy as well as its theoretical and ethical implications are confidently explored: hers is a perspective also informed by the hands-on experience of taxidermic practice, as she prepares her raw materials herself. In the animated video Theatres of Nature, stuffed animals come back to life to re-animate the hidden motivations and assumptions behind the aesthetics of the cabinet of curiosities and the logic of museological display. The highly complex and troubling relationships between the human and the non-human are constantly interrogated in Hood's work, their interface often cast in terms of a face-off. In the eye-catching digital prints of Richard Watson this face-off takes on a glossier but equally unsettling form. Ultra-modern architectural structures become – or are revealed to already be – zoomorphic; a fire burns brightly in a seemingly abandoned, dilapidated living room; dead leaves drown tiled floors; domestic spaces merge with thick forestation. The viewer is what initiated this crisis, whether nature invades

1 'Research at Gray's School of Art', accessed on 26 February 2010
http://www2.rgu.ac.uk/subj/ats/research/home.html,

2 'On the Edge Research Programme', accessed on 27 February 2010
http://www2.rgu.ac.uk/subj/ats/research/initiatives1.html,

the built environment or vice versa but is left with little doubt as to which one will prevail. There is a productive tension between the disorientingly sharp, perspectiveless focus and bright colours of these prints and their evocation of entropy. Watson addresses the 'natural insecurities and curiosities' of humankind with intelligent ambiguity and bold ambivalence. At first glance, Scott Simpson's oil paintings appear to be encased in an irregularly woven wire mesh, or cocooned in a mysterious, organic web: this effect is achieved by matchsticks delicately placed on the painted canvas. Most are landscapes witnessed from afar and, sometimes, from above, from the perspective of a weary rambler, as the artist has suggested. Disturbances of vision, physically induced by the elements and the thickets encountered at conquered summits, shatter the vista into jagged fragments, a jigsaw puzzle that needs to be mentally re-assembled. Yet this fragmentation persists in the mind's eye. The viewed landscape sparks off half-formed memories of previously witnessed scenes, while gaps are partially filled with vision and the imagination: the final picture upholds its integrity by remaining disjointed.

The collaged prints of Gregor Morrison also suggest an embodied perspective on the move, that of a contemporary flâneur and collector of textual and visual ephemera. Morrison mines the overlooked palimpsests of the city, homing in on – and in-between – layers of discarded magazines, instruction booklets, print advertisements. The keenly anticipated developments and artefacts of the recent past are turned into today's trash with a dizzying speed and disconcerting ease. Morrison's prints throw grit in this rapid turnover, slowing down time and shaking the assurance of taxonomic principles that separate commodities from detritus. The aesthetics of his work reference constructivism but his confident refusal to edit brings to mind French New Realism. Mieke Bal has described such images as 'sticky': 'they make you dizzy from the back-and-forthness between microscopic and macroscopic looking where no eyeglasses […] will quite do the job. Looking itself becomes tortuous, almost torturous.'3 The work of Matthew Pang is also decidedly urban, although its subject matter remains deliberately opaque. He combines painting and collage using sharp-edged pieces of Japanese hand-made paper that he colours himself to avoid variables. Some works are covered with viscous layers of dyed glue, at times suggesting slug trails, glimpses through dirty windows or submerged landscapes. Replete with heavily disguised literary echoes, Pang's scenes are often autobiographical and composed from memory but it is their indeterminacy that emerges as their most seductive feature. Legs and bedposts become interchangeable, the raised arms of revellers resemble gently swaying sea anemones, placards from a racist rally suggest a scattering of flower petals or dancing flames. This is a universe of (at least) double vision, where the mundane flickers with intimations of other worlds. Other worlds are what Alice Spicer makes: cut-out swarms of compulsively drawn characters that bear the signature style of the artist and yet remain mismatched, incongruous among themselves. These simple figures brim with personality and hints of disparate narratives that never quite come together. Like runaways from stories that have not been written, Spicer's drawings 'represent a series of worlds – wonderlands maybe, or a series of tiny arguments… silent stories but yet so very loud.'4 As the artist herself has suggested, the act of cutting these eloquent characters away from the white page is significant in its ambiguity: it asserts her authority by retracing

3 Mieke Bal, 'Sticky Images: The Foreshortening of Time in Art of Duration', in Carolyn Bailey Gill (ed.), Time and the Image (Manchester University Press, 2000), p. 99.

4 Alice B. Spicer, The Books They Move by Themselves (Blurb, 2009), p. 36.

the drawn lines with the knife but at the same time grants her creations their independence, which comes at the price of loneliness. The graphic novel is thus deconstructed into DYI kits for visual story-telling. Reflective surfaces have long been used as a strategy for embedding the spectator into the work. Jacqueline Shortland's reflective sculpture in the shape of the letter 'I' aims to heighten awareness of the placement of her work in its exhibition context of New Contemporaries 2010, within the galleries of the RSA and as a designated art object that is viewed by an art public. A mirrored 'I', of course, alludes to the dialectic between self and other (perhaps even Other). Previously standing for the least substantial of graphemes, iota has now become the insignium of infinite customisation in digital gadgetry, as a prefix in lower scale. In English, it is an oft exploited homophone of 'eye' and, in Scotland, 'aye'. A simple but happily resonant concept that reverberates with playful potential.

This is a promising concatenation of images and objects that symbolically underline the entry of Gray's recent graduates into professional art practice. As anthropologist Mary Douglas pointed out, thresholds of all kinds are precarious and anxiety-inducing, and hence often cushioned in ceremony. In the current order of things, becoming an artist is, for once, no more of a gamble than any other path. In this sense perhaps we're all artists now.

ANDY CUMMING

GRADUATED: GRAY'S SCHOOL OF ART

andy.d.c.7@live.co.uk

Robot [2010] Woodcut print, 80 x 100cm

JENNY HOOD

GRADUATED: GRAY'S SCHOOL OF ART
www.jenny-hood.com

Images clockwise from left: **But Not Too Bold** [2009] Digital Print, 42 x 59.4cm; **Theatres of Nature I & II** [2009] Film stills

GREGOR MORRISON
GRADUATED: GRAY'S SCHOOL OF ART
gregor_morrison@hotmail.co.uk

Know How [2009] Screen print and collage on board, 25 x 30cm

MATTHEW PANG

GRADUATED: GRAY'S SCHOOL OF ART

matthewpang88@hotmail.com

The Münster's [2009] Oil on paper

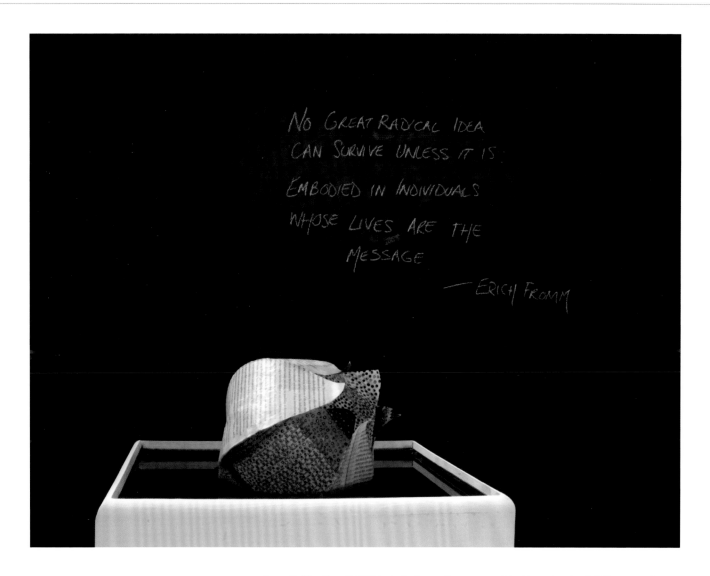

Cross Pollination [2009] Installation - oil, wax, text, blackboard paint, MDF, approx 9 x 9m

SCOTT SIMPSON

GRADUATED: GRAY'S SCHOOL OF ART

simisimpson@hotmail.com

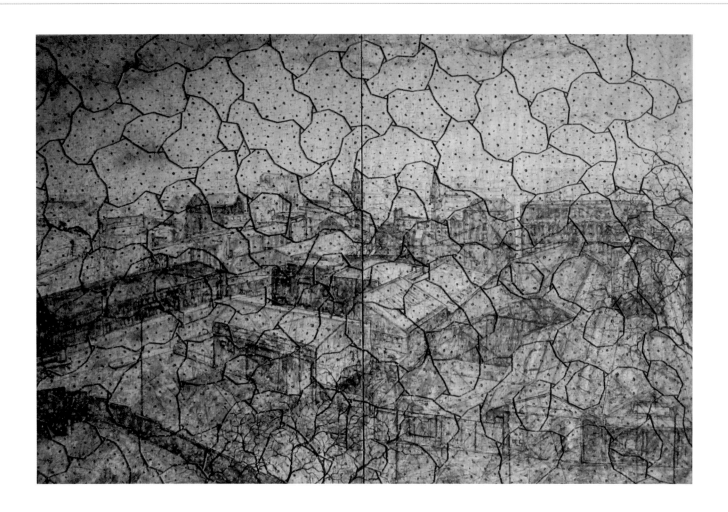

Every Cloud [2009] Oil and mixed media on canvas, 122 x 183cm

ALICE SPICER

GRADUATED: GRAY'S SCHOOL OF ART

alicespicer@hotmail.co.uk

And What remained Was Only Negative Space [2010] Pen and ink cut outs, various sizes

RICHARD WATSON

GRADUATED: GRAY'S SCHOOL OF ART
www.richardwatson.eu

Ceremony [2009] 35mm Digital Print, 83 x 119cm

MORAY SCHOOL OF ART

MORAY COLLEGE, UNIVERSITY OF HIGHLANDS & ISLANDS, ELGIN

FOREWORD BY GINA WALL

ARTISTS

Janet Gordon

Selena S. Kuzman

MORAY SCHOOL OF ART

GINA WALL, CURRICULUM LEADER

Moray School of Art is represented by two graduates, the Slovenian Selena S. Kuzman, and Yorkshire born Janet Gordon. Kuzman currently divides her time between Moray and Slovenia whilst Gordon is based permanently in the Highlands. This diversity reflects the broad range of students enrolled on the Fine Art degree at Moray School of Art where we strive to develop graduates who are creatively and professionally equipped to succeed in a competitive contemporary art environment.

Selena S. Kuzman's video installation $F'(x)=0$ explores opposing aspects of human nature: the Apollonian and the Dionysian. The male and female characterisations of each emerge from the sea to face one another. The continual oscillation of the waves through minima and maxima refers to the infinite transmission of energy. $F'(x)=0$ is the point of intersection between the performers, the fulcrum of dialogue.

The viewer stands at this intersection, the characters' performance pulls our attention from one video screen to the next. Held within this dynamic relation, we are unable to experience the piece in its entirety as each screen faces the other. The viewer is necessarily always in-between.

In $F'(x)=0$, the Apollonian is seen with one's face turned from the Dionysian and vice versa. We might say that our experience of the one bears the trace of the other. The looping film ebbs and flows, it testifies to the dynamism of existence. Life is not essence but a continual play between opposing forces: there is not one without the other.

Whilst Kuzman's video explores dialogue, Janet Gordon's work is a painful monologue which speaks of the emotional consequences of the loss of memory. Gordon's practice is informed by her experience of having a parent with dementia. Her pieces Sitting Room and Everyday are comprised of transcripts of imagined conversations with her mother, those everyday discussions through which we build and nurture our relationships with others.

Sitting Room is a replica of her mother's living space, entirely covered with the text of these imaginary conversations. The discursive space is fixed and stuck to each object. The white paper bristles with the text of a mute conversation. In the corner, the television shows white noise interspersed with fleeting glimpses of Gordon's mother, an image echoed by the words of Roland Barthes:

I never recognised her except in fragments, which is to say that I missed her being, and therefore I missed her altogether. It was not she, and yet it was no one else.[1]

The loss of self caused by dementia is vividly conveyed in Gordon's work, the loved one is torn into fragments like scraps of paper. The cruelty of memory loss poignantly captured by Gordon's phrase: "You remembered that song - word for word, but you didn't remember me."

The engaged and moving work of these two very different artists is testament to the diversity of approach encouraged by our students. We are proud of all of our graduates and the artists chosen for the RSA New Contemporaries 2010 are worthy ambassadors of the school. We wish them well in their respective futures.

---

[1] Roland Barthes Camera Lucida pp.65-66

JANET GORDON

GRAUATED: MORAY SCHOOL OF ART

janet.gordon7@btinternet.com

Sitting Room (detail) [2009] Installation, furniture, paper, 2.5 x 3 x 3m

SELENA S KUZMAN

GRAUATED: MORAY SCHOOL OF ART
www.selenaarte.eu

F'(x) = 0 - Dionysian [2009] Video still

ARCHITECTURE

FOREWORD BY RICHARD MURPHY RSA

EDINBURGH COLLEGE OF ART

Klas Hyllen

MACKINTOSH SCHOOL OF ARCHITECURE

Jonathan Middleton

Jon Morrison

SCOTT SUTHERLAND SCHOOL OF ARCHITECTURE & BUILT ENVIRONMENT

Greig Penny

Sara Russell

UNIVERSITY OF DUNDEE

Cameron McEwan

UNIVERSITY OF EDINBURGH

Piotr Lesniak

UNIVERSITY OF STRATHCLYDE

Andrew Campbell

ARCHITECTURE

RICHARD MURPHY RSA

Forget H G Wells, Isaac Asimov or even Dr Who! If you want to really see into the future then visit the end of year show in your nearest architecture school. Or so it has been said, since what is taught today you might see built everywhere in twenty year's time. Certainly academic trends have influenced generations of architects and certain teachers who may themselves have built little can lay claim to an enormous architectural progeny. So are our six Scottish Schools (soon to be five after the Edinburgh merger) telling us about how we might be living and working in twenty years time; or are they merely holding up a mirror to what is happening today; or even some way behind? Are schools slaves to fashion or can we detect deeper movements? And how relevant are their concerns to what we might consider to be the burning questions of today? Eight students from the six schools are exhibiting in the 2010 New Contemporaries exhibition and as expected there is a huge divergence of activity.

Architecture is a strange activity at the best of times as the architect is always one step removed from the actual process of building. Students are even further removed as they never actually see anything they draw getting built so it's difficult to inject into the teaching process the natural enthusiasm that comes from seeing something you have imagined actually taking shape on the ground. And consequently, within architectural education there are undoubted tensions. Over the years the pendulum swings between on the one hand the idea of the craft-architect, a technical based education dedicated to training in the art and science of how to make buildings and on the other a much more academic and indeed experimental approach encouraging the students to dream the impossible and to present projects which can be completely opaque to the uninitiated. Both are in evidence in Scotland and of course the best schools and the best students combine both.

Not teaching regularly myself, when I am lecturing I sometimes ask the students what magazines they have under their bed. Once the embarrassed laughter has subsided it's interesting to see who is influencing students the most. Ten years ago everything was deconstructivism; Hadid, Gehry, and above all Libeskind were their Gods. Today it seems there is a return to what I might call real architecture albeit overlaid with a strange mystical other-wordly gloss. The Swiss architect Peter Zumtor who has built comparatively little, is undoubtedly a huge figure and students are rediscovering an interest in and enjoyment in the use of materials.

Both the Glasgow School of Art and Edinburgh University take their students to a foreign city (we were lucky to get to Berwick-on-Tweed in my day). Glasgow went to Porto and Barcelona while Edinburgh went to Warsaw and yet the results are very different. From the Mackintosh, Jon Morrison has designed a Museum of Water and Jonathan Middleton a monastery. In the great tradition of the Mackintosh these are seriously complete complex single building designs drawn in a manner that has remained unchanged for decades and revelling in the provocation of inserting a contemporary public building into the fabric of a historic city. The Mackintosh students compete with each other to deliver eye-watering drawings (not surprisingly since so much emphasis is put on the section these are usually a cross-sectional perspectives) but also the School actively encourages their students to deepen their design with technical elaboration. Both these projects are of spectacular buildings, the Porto monastery daring to counter pose itself with the deep valley of the city's topography; the Barcelona centre a massive slab by the side of the street. By complete contrast Edinburgh University students spend most of their time analysing the place, or "reading" it in a manner which many find a tad esoteric. Piotr Lesniak's project is chosen around the theme of the existing Stalinist Palace of Culture in central Warsaw. We are not privy to what it actually is other than a vague suggestion of mass housing. Heroic computer generated images of gigantic semi-complete or maybe semi-demolished city-scapes are presented which while impressive in themselves are incapable of investigation. There's a feeling of enormous energy here, if rather misdirected.

The remainder of the students have chosen projects much closer to home. Klas Hyllen from the Edinburgh College of Art places a literature museum astride the wall of the city's Calton Cemetery. This is a modest scaled project beautifully drawn with evocative images of its interior spaces and how it might sit and draw into it the spaces of the adjacent graveyard and at the same time contribute to the valley of Edinburgh. In fact just the sort of project in a sensitive place that Edinburgh Planners and Historic Scotland would turn down flat! In Aberdeen, Sarah Jennings shows us ideas for a granite museum in the centre of the city neatly combining materiality and place in one project. She's very open about where her influences come from: Zumthor, Hollein, Aalto, Ortner and Ortner and closer to home Neil Gillespie, Gareth Hoskins and yes, your humble reviewer. There are some beautiful photographs of uses of masonry. Her classmate Greig Penny ventures as far as Buckie to locate a community and resource centre on the seafront in an intriguing developing crystalline form, low lying and slightly mysterious in its presence and full of unexpected views both in and out.

Down the road in Dundee, Cameron McEwan ambitiously looks at a Blackness in the city with an exhaustive analysis of the place culminating in a series of modest housing proposals, that attempt to re-urbanise and complete this section of semi-destroyed city. And finally, Andy Campbell from Strathclyde University, turns his back on the familiar city or townscape and addresses his studies to the great suburban fact of East Kilbride

with an analysis of an arbitrary strip through this non-place place. Various markers are proposed in the landscape.

So how do we gather our thoughts? Are there any pointers to the future? What can be said about these graduates who, hopefully, won't acquire the epithet "the lost generation of the recession? "Architecture is a hugely popular career choice for school children, fuelled no doubt by more and more press and TV Coverage. And today it seems students are as diverse as their professional colleagues in their concerns. Projects vary from the modest to the grandiose, from esoteric to almost ready to construct, from socially aware to self-indulgent, with stylistic influences totally catholic. Perhaps diversity itself is a sign of richness. Or maybe students are just looking for a direction. I leave you the exhibition visitor to decide.

Richard Murphy RSA
Architecture Convenor
RSA New Contemporaries 2010

KLAS HYLLEN

GRADUATED: EDINBURGH COLLEGE OF ART
www.klashyllen.com

The Edinburgh Literature Centre. Section perspective through Writers' Retreat looking east [2009] Digital print 520x520mm

JONATHAN MIDDLETON

GRADUATED: MACKINTOSH SCHOOL OF ARCHITECTURE

www.middletonvanjonker.com

Project Title: Monastery on a Cliff, Porto, Portugal. Long Section 1:100 [2009]
Pencil, charcoal, crayon, graphite & photocopy on 90gsm tracing paper, 118.9 x 84.1cm

JON MORRISON

GRADUATED: MACKINTOSH SCHOOL OF ARCHITECTURE
jondmorrison@gmail.com

La Museu de L'Aigua Barcelona' or 'The Museum of Water Barcelona [2009] Images clockwise from left:
Cascading Walls; **Rambla Del Raval**; **Subterranean Reservoir**. Computer generated digital prints

Shifting Pedagogies. Scheme for a Community + Learning Resource Centre, Buckie [2009] Computer generated digital print

SARA RUSSELL

GRADUATED: SCOTT SUTHERLAND SCHOOL OF ARCHITECTURE & BUILT ENVIRONMENT
sara_ddp@hotmail.co.uk

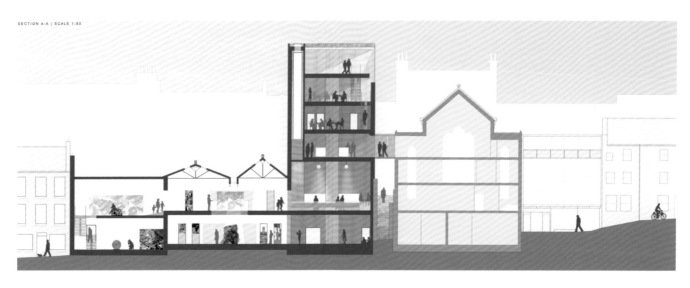

The Adelphi - A granite museum in the granite city. Images from top:
Section through existing buildings and proposed new extension [2008]; **Shiprow Street Elevation** [2008]

CAMERON McEWAN
GRADUATED: UNIVERSITY OF DUNDEE
cameron.mcewan@yahoo.com

The Architecture of Analogy, Blackness. Images from left:
Blackness Forms Sketch Study [2008] Mixed media, chalk, charcoal, graphite and india ink on painted lining paper, 50 x 35 cm.
View of Model from South [2009] Digital photograph, 59 x 42 cm

PIOTR LESNIAK

GRADUATED: EDINBURGH UNIVERSITY

piotr.lesniak@vp.pl

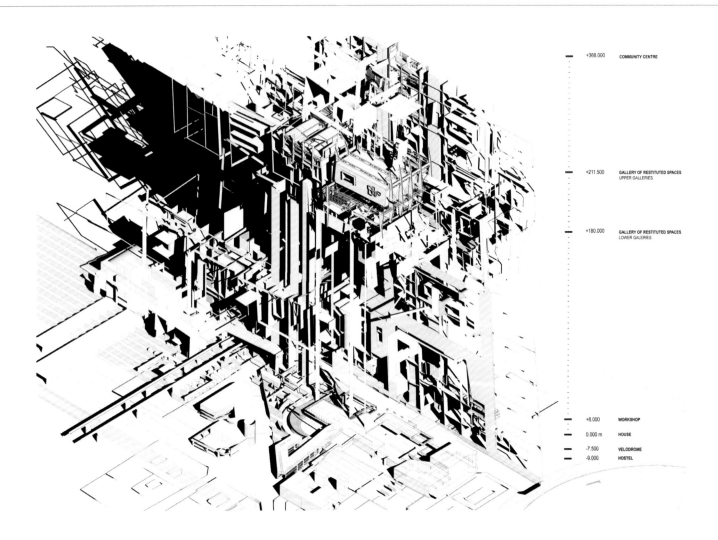

+368.000   COMMUNITY CENTRE

+211.500   GALLERY OF RESTITUTED SPACES
            UPPER GALLERIES

+180.000   GALLERY OF RESTITUTED SPACES
            LOWER GALERIES

+8.000   WORKSHOP

0.000 m   HOUSE

-7.500   VELODROME

-9.000   HOSTEL

Restitued Spaces: A Fold Project for the City of Warsaw [2009] The Fold – Isometric view

ANDREW CAMPBELL

GRADUATED: UNIVERSITY OF STRATHCLYDE
www.dressfortheweather.co.uk

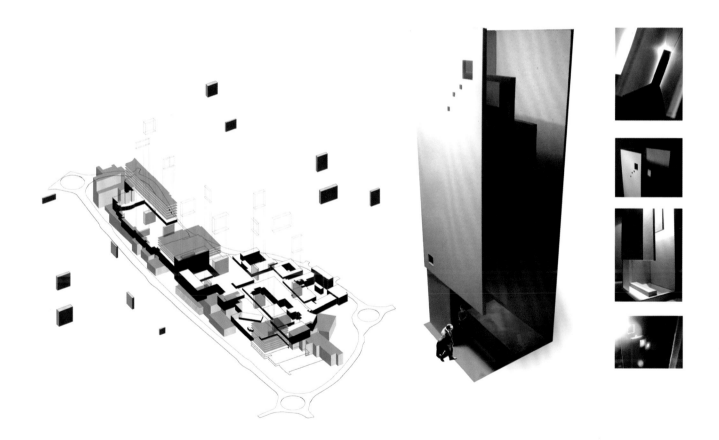

Images from left:
Voids/solids: A series of clock towers [2009] Computer image
Void: East Kilbride Shopping Centre [2009] Model and montage

RSA NEW CONTEMPORARIES
LIST OF AWARDS

The Royal Scottish Academy would like to take this opportunity
to thank all of the award givers at the RSA New Contemporaries
exhibition for the generous prizes and opportunities they offer
in support of emerging artists in Scotland. The following awards
will be presented at the opening reception.

RSA SIR WILLIAM GILLIES BEQUEST AWARD [£2000]

RSA PAINTING PRIZE & THE MACLAINE WATTERS MEDAL [£400]

RSA SCULPTURE PRIZE [£400]

RSA ARCHITECTURE PRIZE [£400]

RSA PRINTMAKING PRIZE [£400]

RSA CARNEGIE TRAVELLING SCHOLARSHIP FOR PAINTING [£200]

RSA ADAM BRUCE THOMSON AWARD FOR ANY CATEGORY [£100]

RSA LANDSCAPE AWARD FOR A DRAWING, OIL OR WATERCOLOUR [£100]

RSA CHALMERS BURSARY FOR ANY CATEGORY [£75]

RSA STUART PRIZE FOR ANY CATEGORY [**£50**]

RSA CHALMERS-JERVISE PRIZE FOR ANY CATEGORY [£30]

THE STEVENSTON AWARD FOR PAINTING [£5000]

HOPE SCOTT TRUST POSTGRADUATE AWARD [£1000]

FRIENDS OF THE ROYAL SCOTTISH ACADEMY AWARD [£500]

STANDARD LIFE INVESTMENTS PROPERTY INVESTMENT ARCHITECTURE AWARD [£500]

Awards continued opposite...

RSA NEW CONTEMPORARIES
LIST OF AWARDS

PEACOCK VISUAL ARTS AWARD FOR MOVING IMAGE
6 MONTHS FREE ACCESS TO PEACOCK'S DIGITAL FACILITY

EDINBURGH PRINTMAKERS AWARD
PRINTMAKING COURSE, MEMBERSHIP AND A STUDIO SESSIONS

EDINBURGH SCULPTURE WORKSHOP GRADUATE RESEARCH AWARD
ONE MONTH WORKING IN ONE OF THE ESW GARDEN PAVILIONS
PLUS FEE, SUPPORT AND FREE MEMBERSHIP

GLASGOW PRINT STUDIO AWARD

THE SKINNY AWARD
EXHIBITION OPPORTUNITY, VENUE HIRE, ASSOCIATED PRESS, PROMOTION AND LAUNCH EVENT
ONLINE AND MAGAZINE PUBLICITY WITH A DOUBLE PAGE SPREAD IN THE SKINNY SHOWCASE

RENDEZVOUS GALLERY/LINDA CLARK NOLAN AWARD
PAINTING RESIDENCY IN LEWIS AND INVITATION TO TAKE PART IN THE
GAELIC CONNECTIONS EXHIBITION AT RENDEZVOUS GALLERY IN 2010

SCOTLAND'S COLLEGES AWARD
AWARDED TO ARTISTS WHO HAVE STUDIED AT A
SCOTTISH FE COLLEGE PRIOR TO THEIR CURRENT COURSE

DAVID & JUNE GORDON MEMORIAL TRUST AWARDS
FOR WORKS BY ARTISTS BORN OR STUDYING IN GRAMPIAN REGION

ROYAL INFIRMARY EDINBURGH PURCHASE PRIZE
SELECTED BY STAFF OF RIE FOR ACCESSION INTO THE RIE PERMANENT COLLECTION
AND SUPPORTED BY HOPE SCOTT TRUST

INDEX OF ARTISTS

ACKNOWLEDGEMENTS

RSA NEW CONTEMPORARIES 2010

The Royal Scottish Academy would like to thank Selena S Kuzman for use of her image to publicise the exhibition. Thanks also to the Hanging Committee: Joyce W Cairns RSA (Convener), Richard Murphy RSA (Depute Convener), Michael Agnew RSA, Michael Docherty RSA, Ian Howard RSA, Michael Visocchi RSA, Arthur Watson RSA, the Exhibition Staff and Neil Mackintosh and his team for their work in presenting the show. Also thanks to the staff of the Art Colleges and Architecture Schools in Scotland for their invaluable input and support. Thanks to Ray Mackenzie, Gina Wall, Jon Blackwood, Euan McArthur, Gordon Brennan, Alexandra M. Kokoli and Richard Murphy RSA for their illuminating essays for the publication. A thank you to Dr Joanna Soden, the Collections Team, Sheena Walker and the Friends of the RSA for their work on The RSA Friends of the RSA School Competition Exhibition 'The Creative Process'; Lara Moloney at The Skinny; and to Kevin Richardson and 21 Colour for their invaluable assistance in delivering the catalogue.

Also thanks to the prize-givers: The Stevenston Trust; The Hope-Scott Trust; The Friends of the RSA; Standard Life Property Investment; Rendezvous Gallery; Linda Clark Nolan; Scotland's Colleges; The David & June Gordon Memorial Trust; Peacock Visual Arts; Edinburgh Sculpture Workshop; Edinburgh Printmakers; Glasgow Print Studio; Royal Infirmary Edinburgh and The Skinny.

We wish to extend a very special thanks to our media partner The Skinny and to 21 Colour, Glasgow for supporting the print of the publication.

Finally, a thank you to all the participating exhibitors - we wish you well for the future and hope that you will remain in touch with us as your careers continue to progress.

Administration by Colin R Greenslade, Gail Gray, Pauline Costigane, Jane Lawrence, Alisa Lindsay, Susan Junge and Emma Pratt. Exhibition Staff: John Biddulph, Andrew Goring, Dorothy Lawrenson, Thom Laycock, Abigail Lewis, Emma Macleod, Julie McCurdy, Martin McKenna, Francesca Nobilucci, Joel Perez, Emma Pratt, Olga Rek and Derek Sutherland.

Catalogue designed by Alisa Lindsay.
Printed by 21 Colour, Glasgow.

Cover image: Selena S Kuzman 'F'(x) = 0 - Dionysian [2009] Video still'

ISBN 978-0-905783-20-8